Abracadabra,

SUNSHINE

Abracadabra,
SUNSHINE

poems

Dexter L. Booth

 Red Hen Press | *Pasadena, CA*

Book design by Ryan Taylor Brideau

Cover Image: "Hyacint Ostara" by Sebastiaan Bremer

Library of Congress Cataloging-in-Publication Data

Names: Booth, Dexter L., author.
Title: Abracadabra, sunshine : poems / Dexter L. Booth.
Description: First edition. | Pasadena, CA : Red Hen Press, [2021]
Identifiers: LCCN 2020038032 (print) | LCCN 2020038033 (ebook) | ISBN
    9781597094474 (trade paperback) | ISBN 9781597092128 (epub)
Subjects: LCGFT: Poetry.
Classification: LCC PS3602.O664 A63 2021 (print) | LCC PS3602.O664
    (ebook) | DDC 811/.6—dc23
LC record available at https://lccn.loc.gov/2020038032
LC ebook record available at https://lccn.loc.gov/2020038033

The National Endowment for the Arts, the Los Angeles County Arts Commission, the Ahmanson Foundation, the Dwight Stuart Youth Fund, the Max Factor Family Foundation, the Pasadena Tournament of Roses Foundation, the Pasadena Arts & Culture Commission and the City of Pasadena Cultural Affairs Division, the City of Los Angeles Department of Cultural Affairs, the Audrey & Sydney Irmas Charitable Foundation, the Kinder Morgan Foundation, the Meta & George Rosenberg Foundation, the Albert and Elaine Borchard Foundation, the Adams Family Foundation, the Riordan Foundation, Amazon Literary Partnership, the Sam Francis Foundation, and the Mara W. Breech Foundation partially support Red Hen Press.

First Edition
Published by Red Hen Press
www.redhen.org

Acknowledgments

Many, many thanks to the editors and readers of the following publications in which variations of these poems have appeared:

Anti-: "Dead Child Poem"; *Ashville Poetry Review*: "Zeitgeist"; *Bat City Review*: "Second Letter to Natalie"; *Blackbird*: "The White Dwarfs," "May 13th, 2012," "Love in the Time of Revolution"; *Connotation Press*: "My Girlfriend Recaps the News While I Try to Write a Poem," "Explaining Sadness," "Explaining Love"; *descant*: "Enoch," "Conversation Starters or Things I'd Never Say to You in Public"; *Ecotone*: "Concerns, After Flipping Through a Dictionary"; *Four Chambers*: "Abstract Infinity, Farewell," "Nothing in Reverse"; *Grist*: "Body Garden"; *Obsidian*: "The Lazarus Project," "Remedios, Flying a Kite"; and *Waxwing*: "How We Make Art," and "Insomnia Poem."

I'd like to also express my gratitude to Andrew McFayden-Ketchum and the teams at Upper Rubber Boot Books and the Floodgate Poetry Series for their dedication to my chapbook, *Rhapsody* (2020), in which the poems "Sanctuary" and "Conversation Starters or Things I'd Never Say to You in Public" also appear. My appreciation also goes out to Danny Lawless and Canisy Press for including the title poem, "Abracadabra, Sunshine," in the anthology *Plume 9 Poetry*.

Deep respect goes to those who have made space in their lives and hearts for the development of these poems. I'm fortunate to call you my friends, teachers, mentors, and peers. Your food, hugs, kindness, conversation, bluntness, love, laughter, tears, edits, direction, and support helped make this book—this is for you: Diana Arterian, Rachel Andoga Loveridge, John-Michael Bloomquist, Allyson Boggess, Malaika Carpenter, Jennifer Conlon, Gregory Donovan, Norman Dubie, Christopher Emery, Todd Fredson, Christian Gerard, Eman Hassan, Mark Haunschild, Natalia Holtzman, Cynthia Hogue, T. R. Hummer, Mark Irwin, Darren Jackson, Richard Jackson, David St. John, Alex Lemon, Luke Johnson, Anna Journey, Douglas Manuel, Hugh Martin, Susan McCabe, Scott Montgomery, Natasha Murdock, Cate Murray, Dustin Pearson, Fernando Perez, Michele Poulos, Josh Rathkamp, Jordan Rice, Gary Sange, Melissa Tse, Sarah Vap, and Kathleen Winter.

Thanks to Kate Gale, Mark E. Cull, Natasha McClellan, and the entire team at Red Hen Press for believing in this book and treating it with such enthusiasm and care.

To my mother and sister: There are no words. Only endless love.

To anyone who has read this far: I see you. You, too, are loved.

Contents

I

II

III

I

First Letter to Natalie

This is how the body transforms,
a sentence dissolved to a word
by the gentle fist of gin,
grit circling the drain, a hyena
hoping to return to itself
through wandering—no,
teeth hoping to return to
the tenderness of your hair. Before I knew you

Before I knew you

I found myself pissing on the side
of the Charles Bridge and thinking
      why can't everything be as wonderful
      as this. How small,
            everything that ends,
like the stars that explode,
scatter like colored sand
from broken vials on a linoleum floor.

We are not in love, but

We are not in love, but

there exists commitment—that is—
a mix between trust, the middle of a bottle,
and a half-written poem I wrote on a plane.
The girl next to me clacked her belt like a swift
hoping to wake two sleepers with the Morse code
of friendship—

that night you were drunk, not in the park but

at the bar. You let me put my hand on your waist
until you realized everyone was watching
everything. I've come to know about you,
and the gold-tipped steeples in that faraway city
where we lived a small life together
as a temporary tribe.

Listen,

Listen,

at night the Žižkov Tower is like your finger
or a piece of my spine—.

Abracadabra, Sunshine

Imagine
the children who are little and far enough away
they measure their lives by the gallons
of dirty water they bring home,
checking their height yearly
against the hulls of abandoned tanks
until they are tall enough to climb in, old enough
to understand that

even the native body is foreign,
even the peaceful mind at war.

I am attempting
to form an argument—

I am attempting to form an argument
done with teeth,

with the tender pressures
of bone grown in gums,
like bullets in the chilled
throats of rifles.

Say, *there is something in the way we touch*
each other, softly, with the palms of our eyes.

This is our narrative. This is our path to the abyss,

The abyss, the individual letter
hidden within the word.

What we signify in being—
always duplicity. What we mean
to say is *not forever*. What we say
when we say

nothing

is the mating of letters, compression of ink
on the pale lip of an envelope,
the tongue, the moisture and
nothing left to hold it:

Or nothing left to hold, the difference between a lover

and a zombie is not the same
as the difference between a soldier and a snowman.
    At the center we are always rotting, always melting into sticks and mud.
    Some kid will come along and use the bones from your arm as a rifle, because
we are meat and water.

Nothing in Reverse

In the silence we talk about films by Godard,
you tell me that you're afraid
that our world is what's left of a set design
for some unwatched film from the '60s.

You are a scarf that has lost its neck
and in terror is fleeing the sunset.
Smoke that is dashing over rooftops,
glancing over its shoulder in fear.

"What if I was Jean Seberg
in another life?" you ask.
"What if our memories are nothing—

just jump cuts and camera tricks?"

Suddenly we are on the roof.
You are naked, except for my coat
around your shoulders.
Though my thoughts are with you,
my body is stumbling
down a long narrow street
somewhere in France.

Nothing in Reverse

In one version of our lives
my body turns to you,
says in French,
"You're a bitch."

In another version
the translation is sketchy
and it's simply, "You're a scumbag."

Nothing in Reverse

Here the film is distorted
and when I turn
to speak, I see only the back
of your head in a 360° circle.

Should I leave the roof to reconstruct
in the safety of your driver's seat?
I am skeptical of the clouds.
They have not moved in hours.

Absent Humidity

There are things that need to be addressed, but delicately,
like a child's denial of stealing cookies before bed.

You are driving. The sun swings overhead,
an old light bulb. I lean my seat back
until I am staring at the ceiling.

Absent Heat

The air in this town is stale, tastes of urine
and honey. This day, like all others, is good
for viewing the sky that sheds its blue skin,
shifts its violet arms
under the clouds, and we drive
into them like returning rain . . .

In the middle of a blowjob, I thought how strange it was
that I was holding your face, sweating
in someone else's bed. All weekend
the floorboards supported my guilt
as I considered the magic of anatomy.

Absent Pressure

How many cells lurch in the body
before the finger can bend?
How strong the neck must be
to hold up my head, even in shame.

Afterwards you lit all the burners on the gas stove with matches.
I filled the fireplace with wood fetched barefoot from the donkey stalls.

You pleaded, "Don't promise me anything. A promise is just a noise, like
a bird call or a toilet running." It is like all noises—
    an interruption of our internal silence.

Absent Love

We made love and I pulled hard at your hair
in the living room. I left to smoke a joint.
You pointed out the chair and desk you'd used
to fuck your ex last winter. You left me

notes all over the bedroom, written
with a quill pen. I threw them
in the fire. They were just words.

They were just words

When it wasn't too cold we'd walk
the donkeys into the city, up past the rows
of houses, lining the road like teeth.
The neighbors spoke politely, but didn't
bother to fence their dogs.
        They circled us like flies.

* * *

Twice, I grabbed for your hand.
The donkeys grew anxious and irritable near the road.
People pulled over to talk and take pictures,
kids afraid, but smiling from the safety of passenger windows.

We ended up in a ditch. We stopped traffic twice.

The tethers caught on our ankles, and for a while we hobbled
on three legs, our shoulders touching.

They were just words

Later, at the dock, I kissed you,
licked the salt water from your cheek,
and you pointed to two bears sleeping separately
on the flotsam, way out somewhere in the water.

Sanctuary

The billboards are set up all over campus,
two-sided, floating like islands between metal poles.
On one side cows hang upside down,
gutted and bled out—

on the other side: Africans
strung from chains, skin raw, filthy, tight
from months of edema, weeks of starvation.
Everywhere crowds circle the billboards like flies,
pointing and snapping photos.
  A woman with a megaphone yells,
      "Save the animals. We can't let this happen again."

        I think of the Danakil
        Depression, with its twenty-five miles
        of salt—the Afar tribe braving the heat
        for white gold, chiseling their fluoride-softened teeth,

wonder if it's true that no one investigates
deaths in Congo.

                    * * *

At the Phoenix Zoo the African Lion sits, dehydrated
with his tongue out. The elephant eats with her back to the crowd.
Flamingos are tagged with numbers, stand
one-legged and oblivious to that history.

A child tries to climb the gate and I whisper,
    "See that one? Number seven?
    That one is named Zimbardo.
    And the small one huddled in the corner—
        they call him Somersett."

* * *

Years ago, in a dream, I was approached by the woman
with the megaphone. She
simply set down the trash bag she was carrying and walked
off into a crowd. I opened the bag
with a stick. Inside—the decapitated body of a calf.

* * *

The guide tells me, "The lion's roar can be heard
from five miles away."

* * *

Now I am watching a Watusi bull
take a piss, wondering if it could be giving birth—
    there is so much water between us. It leans forward.
The guide says,
    "Watusi cattle grow horns up to eight feet across."

I tell Musheerah about Lurch, the Watusi
with the record for largest horns, over one hundred pounds each.

She doesn't believe me, asks how they got there, how
they survive.

How did we get here? There was a time
when kids your age didn't think
white people were real . . .

Pixel Sky (Exterior)

You were drunk and I sat in the parking lot
cutting your hair with the red scissors from your sewing kit.

You had on your favorite dress. The sky blue
one with sequins. It made me think
of when we found it hanging
in a thrift shop. The dress wore dust for months.
The hanger, like a bookmark, held
the shape of all its owners.

We slip into things so easily forgotten.

Easily forgotten

The way you stuck your tongue in the gap
between your teeth . . . maybe there is something between
the ground and the sky. Not the land or the houses
on the horizon. The way the clouds divvy up
the worst of their weight before parting,

like a hug you don't want to back out of
because what is between will fall,
will curl like the peel of an orange
in a pot of boiling water. It was Sunday.

It was Sunday.

The stores were closed.
There was something I wanted to say—
that radio never picked up a station
but you liked the sound of static.
Once, we heard a voice. You worried it was particles of broken lips
         in time, cracked free from the whole. I whispered,

"It's just snow."

My Girlfriend Recaps the News

for James Craig Anderson

When she says *Ohio*, I don't think
of the animal ownership regulations,
the farmer who sets his forty-nine exotics free
then shoots himself in the barn.

Eighteen tigers, nine lions, eight bears, two wolves,

and most of them so afraid they don't move
towards freedom, and are shot
where they stand. The schools are closed.
The cops tell everyone to stay
off the streets—and when she says *Nebraska*,

I am flipping through my notepads,
intent on writing a poem about lynching. She says,
*two girls were found
locked in a kennel, in a trailer home.
There was a mattress . . . animal feces . . . four adults
watching Jeopardy in the front . . .*

* * *

. . . a pumpkin shortage in Illinois.
          Cancer spreading because of planes dropping poison
                    over farming fields. Pumpkin-in-a-can.
Hoarders stocking up on eBay.

* * *

A quote from a friend: "This has jalapeños.
    This is Southwest Cornbread."

* * *

Then a call from Jonathan, who taught me how to fly fish
and set a lure, and is always concerned about me being eaten
by bears, even way out here in the desert. Jonathan,
whose house in Kalamazoo is surrounded by coyotes in winter,
and whose book is always *about to be done*, as if it were
a murder, and he needed encouragement to follow through.

* * *

Note: drink from the beach, your mouth full of kelp and foam,
glass of iced tea, cherry stem, lemon zest, pearl.

* * *

Drawing of a friend as a robot, dog-eared pages with just my name—
    and she says *every fifteen seconds a burglary happens in the US*
    and a man grows a two-hundred-pound watermelon that won't ripen
    and is green all the way through,
    and cocaine increases dopamine
        related to creativity, which is why . . .

I fold bits of paper into footballs, the way we did in middle school,
and my cats chase them around the room like lions after some little boy
in a B-level horror movie, where you can see the zippers under their manes.

And it's midnight now, and rescuers pull
a fourteen-day-old baby from the wreckage of an earthquake
in Turkey. And I start my poem:

Sunday, June 6 in Brandon, Mississippi . . .

Little Circles

for Bristol, age three

1. Exercise in color and overlapping images

The tongue is a stealthy weapon,
     and your dog's hung over its teeth
like a snake making its way into the sun—
plum-hued in the dark, cherry-fleshed in the light.

I held your dog's rubber ball, contemplating
the little things circles do: ending sentences,
beginning wars, pulling us around
the violent coal of a star.

You found me where your mother left me,
shuffling the hallway near your aunt's bedroom,
counting the items to be moved: the mattress,
makeup kits, the powder-pink bear
and bras. You were naked and white except
the tomato juice smeared on your chest—
     your nipples tiny and pointed as the eyes
     of a wolf cub hiding in snow.

After your bath you stood in the door with your panties
at your ankles, shouting
     look, these are clean!
as your dog chased its tail.

2. Multiple Divisions

In the Great Rift Valley there are soda lakes,
corrosive to human skin. Pockets of magma
send up bubbles—earth below
whispering to earth above. Slowly
everything divides. When the water recedes
the fish break into groups, cichlids infiltrating
schools, getting in close enough to feed
on their neighbors' scales.

This life is division.

Somewhere there are white flamingos
posing as grounded clouds, their heads
tucked through the slit screen of water,
tongues separating algae from rain.
Those tongues will make them pink
once the beta-carotene kicks in—pink
        as a baby's cheeks,
                pink as flesh exposed, without skin.

3. Color Absence

Two years later and I am separating
        olive pits, remembering
that frying pan-shaped city where you live,

my car spinning, the tires in orbit, wild
and dark as your mother's eyes.

I told you the beginning of a fable—
        the witch patiently stirring the cauldron,
the things she adds for flavor: baboon knuckles,
an obsidian ring, bear testicles with the fur stiffly
attached. She waits for an eclipse,
hunts for the little girl lost in the throat
of a cave. The cave is magic.

Please remember all that I have told you,
        even if most of it is a lie.

Three days and the girl grows old and blind.

Loneliness. Speak Through Me.

Who are you? Who am I? Haunted
By the dead, by the dead and the past and the
Falling inertia of unreal dead
Men and things.
—Kenneth Rexroth

Am I to say this heart skips like a gazelle,
or that loneliness taps its walking stick against
my ribs? Blood pumps
like the muscled legs of a horse and I am
large—a blade of grass
under your moon,
hanging like a fractured skull.

Loneliness. Speak Through Me.

Should this end *the rose*
blooms, spreads open
with the weight—of beauty
in the shape of . . .

you should stop reading.

Sorrow is so often camouflaged
by the body—the body grows
dumb and cool.

If this should end, *we found the bird*
with a broken beak, missing wing
I wonder
if this can go on—*please,*
stop reading.

Loneliness. Speak Through Me.

After finishing *In What Hour*, I dig a hole in the yard. They say apes laugh like humans, but they can do it inhaling and we cannot. A friend saw a truck swing open its door; the driver kicked a pregnant dog from the passenger seat and drove away. A sick child once asked me, "How long will the hurting last?" and I spilled coffee on my ivory shirt.

Loneliness. Speak Through Me.

I try on the language of forgiveness
when there is nothing left to say.

How can I translate water?
Two million lotus flowers, still
no snow.

Dead Child Poem

Some days she asked if we could just cut horses out of construction paper.
She would outline my hand, cut violently around the pencil line. I drew
a saddle. Graphite bales of hay. We ripped a paper plate to clouds—

* * *

she wrote this story. I imagined

an umbrella opening its lips above us, but there was no water,
only cotton and latex paint. I was the sky in her box of crayons,
she was the hand that poised me.

* * *

What mattered most were the stories—
I didn't care much for the names, but
the city of stick men and women was
a good place to rest. She understood
death. The black rain cloud over the city,
the red bowls of blood under the people's oval heads.

There was a drawing of your dog, a box
with stick legs and a purple tongue.

And this is really about the tongue,
this poem. The only thing that keeps me alive—
the idea, with its tired spleen and nervous system

pumping my tongue, squared and frosted
against the window. Her eyes, yes
I remember her eyes, winking
in fathoms of snow. Her face
like a star burning away, a bright wound
on the neck of night.

The White Dwarfs

for Chris

I want to believe the Aztecs,
that once you eat the heart of a dragon
you can understand animal language.
I want to believe that the Andromeda galaxy
is just a mirage, like love.
Today someone has been crying
in the house across the street. Someone
is masturbating just up the road,
right now. They sound the same

to me. We aren't that different from the cicadas
or the Century Plant; all we do is die. The sounds
we push out into the universe take their time to arrive.
Just yesterday the radio waves we've been shooting
out into space since the '50s reached the corner
of our solar system. Somewhere a boy is just beginning puberty,
his bones mimicking the slow stretch of the universe.
When he speaks in his sleep tonight he won't notice
the small crackling in his voice. A new word
grows old. Time slips its hands in our pockets
and laughs. It happens again: I started by writing

the story ends with your brother Matt
peeling the tabby from the pavement
        the skull crushed
        the spots on its stomach
little constellations

a name

The body
milk-warm

he places it on the sidewalk

can't look at his date

She says
I think that's my cat
I think that's my cat
and knows

Then the lightning. Then, the long drive home
where you pass the remains of a car with its passengers
burned to death inside. The year of sleeplessness,
night terrors and waking to women you don't love,
your ex still possessing your bones. This is an apology.
Because in Thailand a monk gathers boys
from the sex trade and sells them to miserable
bastards here in the West. Because Kamajors behead RUF soldiers
in Sierra Leone, and RUF cut off Kamajor hands and dicks,
spike them on poles and parade the streets. In China
poachers kill endangered tigers, make Viagra from their bones.
You complained we are not here to be happy, and I agree

this is what we do: drink alone at dive bars
reading Bukowski, crying for the woman raped on the reservation
who can't tell her friends. Once you were so drunk
you pissed on a stranger's lawn, looking in through the window
at the family. Once a brunette sat down at the table with us
and barked. Where does this lead? That poor woman. If only
the cat didn't have spots, or she hadn't seen it lying in the road.
If only her father hadn't died a week before, and maybe if your brother
had known just what to say.

Yesterday, someone smashed my car window,
but only stole a pair of shoes from the back seat. Yesterday you woke
with a pain in your chest, coughing up black phlegm
and afraid your mother is going blind. Look what we do to ourselves,
slipping a chloroform rag under our noses,
lacing our love with PCP. All we can do is survive,
like the boy in a Syrian home, found days after an operation to retrieve corpses
from a massacre. He hid beneath the bodies of his parents.
How he must have cried. You cried the same way
the night the doctor avowed your brother would be a vegetable.
After two hits of acid cut with PCP, Matt threw himself through a window.

This world is beautiful, only because of the massive black hole
pulling all our light into its heart; only because the scrub jay,
witness to its own mortality, sings in alarm for its dead
until it is joined around the body in a prayer only understood
by the ash of the forest, stretching away from its origin.

Like our universe, it will soon collapse.
Let us die dreaming—pretending we will go on forever,
voices large as the Terra Cotta Army in the tomb of Qin Shi Huang.
Let us be the paint that evaporates from their faces.
Let us be that dust.

Second Letter to Natalie

My favorite story is the one you tell at parties, about your mother:
how after the divorce she brought the mini fridge up from the basement
and spent her nights locked in her room with a video of her wedding
on a loop. How you skipped school, snuck into the room once with Eric Tenyson,
the student tutor for algebra trig, because he promised you could cheat
off his final in exchange for a fifth of Grey Goose and a blowjob.

Really, he was a bartender. You had short hair he might have grabbed
like a handful of sand, and we were never children, though I tell the story this way:
the fridge was spare but for three cucumbers, and what you thought was a shoe box
of home videos was actually full of condoms. A box,
you asserted, that was open and trembling in your hands.

Maybe you would describe the door clapping like your lips
around his cock as Eric left you to bask in the knowledge
that you would always be just as lonely as your mother.
And as desire sank its teeth into your neck
You would handle the vegetable like a pearl. You would
wet the tip but couldn't tell your mother
why you could never eat a salad again.

But he was a bartender, and I don't tell that story
these days because I promised to keep your secret
the way my mother keeps all those shitty drawings
of horses and Nazis I made in fourth grade.

Natalie, this morning the sun rose
like a body—not Jesus,

but the pigeon a friend witnessed,
as cloud-white as semen, its entrails teased out
like warm mozzarella in the beak of a gull, and

I thought of the blind violence of friendship;
the hurt in a hug, the letting go.

I scribbled on a napkin:

What I give to you comes from my hands, the wrinkling
of vinegar on paper. The stars hanging themselves
every night—they come for me.

Back here in the desert the bars close
well before dawn, and my eyes grow frosty with whiskey
as I look into bathroom mirrors. They are windows—every window
you can remember, with its sorrow wax-melted
under cold city lights, a cavern built into the chest of your grieving body.
The wind flutters through it sometimes
with enough force to match the Tevatron, to smash
the atoms of our solitary lives, and for a moment make us believe
there is more to life than the buffalo, the four-mile tunnel,
dark and empty as the sky on the morning
Jeffrey Dahmer was baptized, under the stygian eye
of a solar eclipse.

Natalie, these are things that loom over our lives—

brushing my teeth, I imagine I am Roy Ratcliff,
holding Dahmer under until his body goes
still, until the angels howl like wolves in redemption,
until his face goes soft in my guilty hands, and the sour water
is a screen that flattens your eyes. That warm embrace that says,

I'll miss you, where are you going from here?

I brush until my gums bleed. I try
to stay rooted in a dream where there is an earthquake
in Virginia. My mother is slicing cucumbers as the world spreads.
You, you are telling me again that you might be pregnant
as we drink a stranger's homemade liquor in the hall, as you again
describe the Boy Scouts in lemon-colored hats that followed you for days,
as though they could smell the bartender's sweat on your neck.

Even after these months, with you so far away and shining with shame,
I imagine colored feathers falling from the sky wherever you walk.
When you spoke of him I could see the angels shuffling
in the pit of your heart (as though it were a flooded dance floor).

I recall an article I read about water
in the Great Rift Valley. How it has so much fluoride
it softens the teeth. And the Afar tribe, to mark their resilience
and resistance to pain, chisel them
to a fine arrowhead point, and stalk the desert, which

somewhere is made of salt so white
it stretches into the distance like the train on a wedding dress.

I gargle and spit, stare in the mirror long enough
that I swear I can see my beard growing.

The night before your second date
I tested the smoothness of your thigh with my palm,
and we passed a bottle of vodka around
like an offering of lamb.

In Prague,
it felt as though the city devoured everything,
was a white hole regurgitating history
like bad Chinese food with whiskey,
making constellations that chart the human drive—desire.

I regret not seeing the drawings the children made
at Terezín. I missed the trip to the camp, and instead
watched tourists in Malostranské Square ride
their Segways across the Charles Bridge.

Before you remind me, I am still working
on your letter, but that night at the Czech-Chinese restaurant,
when I touched a plastic spoon,
wiped Sriracha into my eyes,

I thought for sure my body was taking revenge
for the way I looked at you

while we were drinking. You laughed.
The other customers left humored and full. But
                    I stepped out into the night, swollen and unmoved.

II

May 13, 2012

for Jordan

Today America wakes like a toddler,
rubbing the crust of Saturday from its eyes to find
forty-nine decapitated bodies along the road
to Nuevo Leon. Limbs in trash bags. 3:00 a.m.
sunlight sliding into the horizon.

I stand in the yard while a dragonfly
lands on the tip of my car antenna.
      The bloody show begins,
again. Your wife is in labor.
There is no song to capture this day.

* * *

I go alone to water the vine tomatoes.
Heat has hugged the life from the leaves:
      such accidents come from love.
One ripe and ruby-hued globe has survived,
hangs, a planet in a field of debris.

      Soon the vines will be dust.
      Summer starts the process
        of slow devouring.

* * *

Everything changes: you tell me
you are transgender, your body and mind are
separate animals that cross paths, but do not touch.
        What can you say to your wife, or to your mother
whose only word is *no*—
                the socket of her mouth like a fist of coal,
                        burning deep inside your throat.

Perhaps I will meet a woman,
you say. She might be drunk
after half a glass of wine, laugh
at my jokes, smile with her whole face,
as real as the cracked dirt loaded over graves.

                        * * *

        This time next week there will be an eclipse
        like nothing we have seen since childhood.
        The moon will shove its bald head between
        us and the sun, stay lodged there for a lifetime
        of breaths, as a secret . . .

And on the phone you're saying her name:
Denise. The imaginary woman I'll marry. She'll tell me
I'm extremely sweet,
as the dark ingests the city and I reach for her hand.
Then in the pitch I'll recall the end of "Happiness" by Robert Hass—
        in bed kissing, / our eyes squinched up like bats

and I'll forget her, and remember December,
my mother coming home, Christmas gifts from the church:
trash bags of dismembered doll parts, incomplete card decks,
crayons without names.

* * *

I will cry,
because even through a pinhole the moon will look like the head of a baby
crowning, the ring of blood like fire, a thing
dangerously fascinating to the eye. The baby will be jaundiced—
drink and cry and drink. I'll drink and cry just the same.
        All that blood, and more . . .

When I call my mother she reminds me
my grandmother has died. My cousin Shirley Mae
has died. Alexandra and Kyliyah Bain are alive, but
motherless, as we all eventually are, but

she has a boyfriend. My mother
no longer goes to bed alone. Though every morning
she calls and I am still her one son.

She limps to work
to push an elderly woman
                        who can no longer walk.
She limps to the post office, limps

to the mirror and ignores the conflicts of the body:
  what she can no longer produce: hair,
    teeth.
It was not until my grandmother died that I heard her say
she loved me, that I am still her only son,

        her only boy.

                    * * *

Why does it feel so unnatural to be this—
    not a father, not yet . . . not anymore . . .

I say *parent* and I watch you hold him,
I say *Jonathan* and I mean the person you used to be.

Already, your son reaches for your breasts
that are rising like heat off the pavement
at noon. You want to feed him. Your jaw is thinning.
People are asking questions, so you hide
like Apollo on the day of Phaethon's death.

But the moon slides loose from the clouds—
    a head rolling to the feet of an assassin,
        smiling at this separation from the body,
            this chance to become something new.

Even by Skin

I don't use red ink on my students' papers.
Though many words are misspelled.
I patiently explain how to conjugate verbs. I quote
Babel: "No iron spike can pierce a human heart
as a period in the right place."

I tell them six months ago, an alcoholic tattooed Rilke
on my forearm. I couldn't smell his breath
or see that he didn't recognize the words,
kept his fist over the stencil until a fault was done.

What had he known of this elegy? He must have
mistaken the English for German. What else
could have explained the language of blood
raising error on the skin?

After Collaging Letters from Imaginary Girlfriends

After your mother
has counted the garlic,
missed two because the dog is gnawing them
beneath the table, after you have cut your tongue
sealing the envelope
you will send to Guam, tea stain
your signature along the back,
rub a little basil along the edge
for luck. Let it sit

in the drawer, wounded. Let it sit
until you need it, need it
like fucking a stranger
in a short, tomato-red dress,
her tongue of escaping
balloons, lips of peeling paint
flaking on your neck.

Dear, your palm is small and cold,

familiar. Like the smell of pot,
of beer smeared on necks
like cologne.

How We Make Art

I spent the morning painting
cardboard trees. Jagged spears
that did not lay well
under the mouth of scissors.

I mangled the beer box

until there was only a forest of rockets
and bombs displaying alcohol
labels under thin films of acrylic.

The horizon is sharp and angled
now. I've planted corrugated pine in the living room.

At sunset they look like searchlight cones,
mini drag beams from an army of UFO abductions,
tepees made of flayed alien skin, anything

but your eyes

returning to point and say what you see is
growing dull now that you've been
probed and abandoned
in the dark woodlands of memory.

She said, "A is for orchard,"

and she meant it. "A garden
is like a city with the buildings
ripped up from the ground."

She meant everything.
The vertical tilt of her head let me know
that she couldn't be real.

She liked sweet potatoes and '80s sci-fi films,
classic rock and sex without condoms.
She had a little bit of every woman I've been with
and it scares me that she kissed with her eyes
open, breathed through her nose, tried to ingest my chin.

I dream that she planted saliva eggs in my beard
and they hatched turnips.

I might be going insane.

She thought men shouldn't take baths,
people should always pee alone
because we aren't like other animals—
    "We're so stupid, we get attached."

Her cat pranced by with its nose in the air.

* * *

Revision: She had a gluten allergy
and an affinity for smart guys because
they gave her what she called a "brain boner."
She ate Hungry Man dinners and smoked Camel Menthols.
Her hips were hyper-mobile, which is actually a bad thing in the bedroom.

From the look of a plant she could tell me that it was a rubber tree
and it reminded her of my skin when I was nervous.

Revision: what she really whispered was
"P is not for pussy," then uncrossed her legs
and smiled . . .

Blueprint of Our Last Conversation

You left a blade of dead grass
on the seat of my car. I fashioned
your studio table with two plastic
loaves of bread. It was not enough.
Your palms netted like a sieve
as I cast my shadow from the line,
waited for you to trace it
with your tongue, fill it with color
and sap, impossibly corrugated
birdseed.

You passed. Your hair was far too clean
a brush for painting my figure, my hands too frail
to nibble when they weren't wrapped around
your ankles. You hissed,

This doesn't concern me.

Empty smile, like fresh blown glass.
Marble eyes made of wood and bone.

It is only for the river mud and cold . . .

If not you, then who will save me

Winter, an oddly warm rain,
my worries written out
on the back of a grocery list,
folded in my sock.

For months I read comics about robots,
pigtailed avengers and caped squirrels.
I could not have been less aware
of the earth sliding beneath me,
or your breasts pushing up
    like mountains.

How badly you wanted
to run away with your mother's earrings;
the only thing she ever really had to give you.

I was there in my crooked glasses.
I watched her fingers curl around cigarettes
as though they were your throat.

Tiny hands nailed to the stainless steel crosses;
the markers of thirteen years of guilt.

* * *

When our neighbors weren't home
we broke in the back door

because you wanted
a romance of strangers.
We took a bath in their tub,
drank tea by candlelight,
touched everything but the portraits
hung in the living room.

You left the water running.

Nina, I heard you coughing. In the dark
the ribbons on your pigtails were flags
I followed in that house
we wandered through like a forest.

Body Garden

for Carlene

1.
Why you hated lilacs I will never understand.
All winter the buds set about their drooping
like workers on strike—suddenly human—
    wrecked by despair.
Cold, and colder still. The city huddled
  for months under angry clouds. The wind,
with all its secrets, lashed the trees bare
until even the roots trembled in the soil.

    We all make sounds no one wants to hear.
In the next apartment a woman is taking a bath,
singing Dolly Parton. It could be summer,
if not for the frost spreading its web
across the window, the birds calling to each other
that the nuts are stiff, settle in the stomach like stones.

And here I am
    writing you this poem, days after the first desert rain
because your handwriting reminded me of my mother's
and because you said everything with such a lack of compassion
I wanted to believe it was true.

2.
When your roommates fucked, you said you could hear them,
her screaming, like a tea kettle ignored. You said you'd never

been touched like that, with such tenderness and attention.
Is that why you worked with your hands—to feel nothing
but cold clay under your nails?
Is that why you labored to dig bottle caps from mud,
reading the labels with a thick German accent,
hoping for my laughter, wine-induced and honest?

How often you wanted to be a maple, important and connected
to the world, holding the bluebird, beetles nesting
in your palms.

3.
We were looking for the same thing: a reason to say no
to the sunset, to the jeweled sky that left its residue on the hills.
You wanted the shadows and I, the comfort
found even in the hands that made garbage of the river.

Forget all the nights you spent teaching me to dance,
the floor shining like ice under the strobe light. The frowns.
The clicking heels and tongues. Forget your father,
bald and curious about everything but my name.
Forget that you told me I only taught you how to want
and want more.
  Rain weight, you said.
      Pebble compression,
        and so on.

Enoch

The night you pointed to the mountain and said
    I need to go conquer my demons
I dreamt of the Lion Man of the Hohlenstein Stadel
being licked clean by a lamb. On its tongue and between its teeth
the lamb carried the tawny fur, that dander
slick as the ivory from which it was sculpted.

I dreamt I saw your face
on the body of that lion

and I was afraid. Whenever you went on a binge
your blood sugar spiked, everyone worried
you were giving up one of your ghosts. Guilt:
a force even the body can't defend.

At church they taught you it was evil
to think carnally of a woman.
Quarter in a jar each time you masturbated—
offerings for sin. You tell me

you've met a black dominatrix in Virginia, but
you won't say you want her just for her skin,
as if she were some animal
in bed who you knew could break you.

These are things saviors do, and
you are a savior, no? Your sex brings women

back from the whorehouses clean and virginal. You say
    minnows and *prayers for my father,*
    I am
    my father
    in this death, Amen.

The vernacular of the divine
Latin, wet and growing hard
on the tongue like nipple—flesh
puckering, prayer permanently smearing
prophecy on the poor.

I don't know your Bible, nor will I
pretend. The snake you brought down from that mountain
was dead and had three heads: one for each of your vices.
On the ride back the car was a boat. Kharon, you led us down
into Tempe and you left us: that's the story you tell,

but you say it
this way: *at least I ain't brown.*

That kind of relief is like pissing
on the back of a woman whose skin was boiled
by the sun—the accident, a half-god's failure free fall:

Something no one wants to appropriate.

After your visions of S. drowning himself in the lake you visited
Kutnah Hora, spoke with the forty thousand people whose bones decorate the
Chapel.

Na zdravi!

Who cares if the cup is filled with mead or blood? The ego goes down harsh,
with a burn.

What the Moon is Not

1. Sclera

A pearl spinning in the endless throat of the universe,
the whites of a god's eye, without iris,
without fear. The moon is not the heart
of a match plunged and quickly cooled in a glass,
not the silver refuse of clouds,

the de-shelled meat of a coconut,
or a marble, a peephole knifed
in the dirty sheet of night.

2. Iris

In a letter Lowell wrote,
     Regard people as glass
spheres, filled with stained water . . .

I do this with hesitation, sinking
into the cupped palm of the bathtub.
I like to think of myself as the ring
my body will leave behind, beads of scum
on the porcelain, childhood filming over
what's left like fog,
          and in that fog the night slips over me
                    as oil over water, the oil aflame,
                    the water a window dissolving
                    into summer . . . *gradual suffusion forming*
                              the space between . . .

Explaining Love

for R.A.

We left the Christmas party and you said,
    It's cold as a witch's tit,
and I promised to use it in a poem. Here it is.
I won't lie and say that I wasn't thinking
of your nipples then, iced erect under your blouse.

I am not flirting with you. I tried that once. Now
I am only being human. You drove me home
and I wondered if friendship is a type of love
separate from desire.

Explaining Love

It may be years before you read this,
decades before you understand. One day,
little sister, I might be your only friend.

This is in our blood.

I wish I had known sooner
that Mom's back ached for months
before our grandmother died.
Before I left for college,
when you were too small
to help, we lifted her up the stairs
because she could not walk,
though her ghost leg said *touch* to her brain,
itch to the few fingers she could still move.

I saw her naked, bathed her, and I am not ashamed.

In Thailand, little sister, workers take ya ba
and stay up for days, knowing how it ruins the body,
so that they can make money for their families.

This is sacrifice. I can't say it any other way.

Explaining Love

for my students

I tried explaining that we are just another set of animals
with needs. Dying is what we do best,
when we are least shy; alone.

I said, "We bury each other with our hands,
mourn with our eyes." Our voices
grow soft in fire—

I cannot teach you this.

What you put on the page is not
what you feel in your heart, it is
filtered through words—
that might be too much
to start with.

Neruda wrote, "Love is short, forgetting is so long."

If nothing else, I want you all to know
   gin is not the same as blood. A poem
about cocktails and ovaries is not an elegy,
nor is it funny.

I once loved a girl
     I met in a hospital.
For a while we had matching pirate tattoos
and when the nurses weren't looking

I inked a promise ring on her pinky,
told her I'd buy her a horse to replace
the one her parents owned when it died.

On a Thursday she hung herself
with a bed sheet, broke every capillary in her neck,
and for two weeks could not talk, and so wrote
letters to me on playing cards.

Her face was a kind of blue you don't see
in nature. She thought it was funny,
wrote: *I look like the last berry*
on a juniper tree.

Elegy for Los Alamos

In winter the tree house was bare
and cold. The termites had invaded
and eaten through the floorboards
twice that fall. Frost built around the holes
on the branches, the windowsill.
There was no glass
so I held your ankles while you hung
out and picked the icicles from
from the furthest limb, careful not
to snag your sweater on the rusted
nail where we would hang our flags.

That winter would last a decade. We thought

the ice would never melt.
January we slept
with our cheeks to the shrinking wood
every night after flipping through
your dad's *Playboy* collection.
He brought an undated calendar from the factory and
we spent a week eyeing naked blondes.
The pages were wrinkled and smelled
like whiskey. You confessed that was the smell
of change, the smell of an early

spring. We both hid
our embarrassment because

I had never seen a naked woman
and your father didn't know
the son that he was raising.

On the cover
a woman held a breast in each hand
and the words over her head
read "Come Meet Little Boy and Gadget!"
Her hair and teeth—so bright
we couldn't look into her glare.

Concerns, After Flipping Through the Dictionary

W is for wamble: a turning of the stomach,
my face green as sea foam when I am sick
with anxiety, can no longer watch the news
or listen to my cats howl for supper—things I ignore:
    the bald spot on my head,
    the nervous jerking of my hands,
    the pea-sized lump under my left armpit
    (which I swear is stress)
    that warns me I am young, too young
to be worried about aging and losing teeth

like my mother. I'll tell you this: a lizard stole my cats' food
for a month before I noticed, and, being from the city,
I had never been so close to the desperation of nature.
I wanted to kill the poor thing . . .

Question: what animal is more sensitive than man?

I read today that in India a twelve-year-old drank
Thyodine and died. Her father was going blind
and her brother's kidneys were failing, and
she left a note that said *give my eyes and kidneys to them.*

Sometimes I want to drown myself in the waters of Lethe,
go back to when I was nothing but blood
rising in my father's penis, not even capable of hope,
not knowing abandonment—

and in my misunderstanding of fear I called Cate,
who scooped up the lizard and took it back
into the safety of the wild gravel and desert
of our front yard . . .

And to think, this started with a letter.

When I was in Prague, from the skate park on the hill, behind the cherry-colored metronome, I could see the city from the sky—the way it was meant to be. The gold-tipped statues and the oxidized copper of the cathedral steeples set aflame by the setting sun, the silver mirror of water bending the Charles Bridge like the twisted limbs of break dancers at the edge of the park, or the strings of shoes knotted low over sagging phone wire. Milos said the statue of Stalin once stood headless there, and when he was toppled, with his arms spread open, he wanted to take the whole city with him.

W is for wanion: ill luck or misfortune.

The girl in India was cremated before her note was found.

After my girlfriend broke up with me,
we saw a dead quail under the bridge

and John said,
This is everything. We were staring west,
with the river to our backs,
observing the dry pit, with its runoff from the city,
small patches of vegetation. I wanted
to reach out, pull the corner of sky over my head

because all I could think about was Sunday night,
her whispering "manscaping," hand on my cock,
the hairs between my legs curled around her
pinky and ring finger. Even if I pleaded she wouldn't

wear a dress because they made her feel awkward,
wouldn't keep her shirt or socks on while fucking
because she loved the sound of skin on skin, because

"It's like lying on your back and listening to waves."

I returned to the water the next day, and maybe it was that sunset,
but I couldn't find the quail, in the same way
I searched for her eyes but only heard her
say from the darkness *some things just disappear.*

Explaining Sadness

For my birthday, Scott brought me a boomerang
he found in an alley, and I tucked it into my belt,
strutted around the bar until they kicked me out
for having a weapon in my pants.

At home I hung it on the wall,
thought of the little girl who might have thrown it
sitting at the window every night, waiting
for it to return, like her father, who told her before leaving
that accidents only happen to the careless and ignorant.

I once slammed my sister's finger in the car door.
Maybe I meant to. During last month's storm
an oak fell into my high school English teacher's living room.
No one pointed a finger at the tree. A neighbor told his daughter
the tree got tired and needed to lie down.
That night his daughter dreamed of being knocked over
and not getting back up—
of being swallowed into the earth.

I miss the hills of the graveyard, swollen with gravestones that were never made
because the families of the dead couldn't afford them.
I say this to my mother and I know
there is nothing to do but pace the room
until I have caught up with my shadow and the feedback
on the phone is the sound of my first girlfriend singing

in the shower. Tonight, I'll take any distraction.
I'll listen for any creature that cries because of the sunset,
to any drop of water that thinks it is independent
enough to leave its mother
in search of the river. We make our own canyons

if we drag our feet long enough, and if we refuse to move
and are impaired by depression, death sneaks up
on its four spindly legs and rips us from our body
like a sheet of notebook paper. Little girl,

we know each other only by this chunk of wood, but I still imagine
you waking, your hair folded over your shoulders
like the wings of bats, crying because you are afraid of the future,
its toenails growing beneath your bed.
If we ever meet I'll confess that I've been having the same dream

for the last ten years: a friend falls asleep and has a seizure,
chokes on his vomit. His mother holds my hand—
that drop of water makes its way to the ocean,
leaves its trail on the beaches Sierra Leone and Kudu
where the rain is good luck, and the amputees walk
with their heads down to see the diamonds from the mud.

Conversation Starters or Things I'd Never Say to You in Public

for R. A.

False: Napoleon didn't shoot off the nose of the Great Sphinx of Giza.
The truth is humbling: the Sufi Sheik, Sayim al-Dahr blew up the nose
because, of course, *any statue of a negro's face that large*
must have been idolatrous.

These are my thoughts on Halloween night,
two-thirds into a bottle of Syrah, twenty thousand miles
from home, and dressed in zombie latex that
only came in two shades of Caucasian. All this glue
and the wounds won't stick. All this fake
blood and brown Sharpie so I can tell
everyone I am a dead black guy
resurrected by the White Man Virus,
and you'll laugh.

At the end of the night Christine's friend will
take photos on the porch, after a moment
of focusing his camera say, "I can't see you,"
to which I'll respond.

That, sir, is racist.

It is a joke. It is a Sufi Sheik-Napoleon cannon-bomb
that has nothing to do with height, the number
of men you've seduced, the fact
that our lives are just expansion
and cooling; we are

the after-effect of the Big Bang.

But I digress,
        it is dark, and I am drunk.
I am drunk and you, dressed
as a bridesmaid, wearing six-inch heels.
It is dark and we are friends
and I am inebriated enough for it to be
awkward that your breasts are
where I am used to seeing your eyes.
You, suddenly my height, and still
pleasant. So unlike Stripper Nick,
who will later say
he is going to college in CA to major
in brewing beer. Less than a year ago
he was one of two men fighting for your
bed in a bar parking lot.

And there's Fernando
who two years past
dressed as a banana
but tonight is a panda
or a Hispanic guy in black face,
all excessively sexual
depending on your B.A.C.
        and sense of humor.

This of course returns
to the dark. Scientists say that
if the universe keeps growing
outward the notion of a star
will be millennial mythology.

Imagine looking up and thinking
        the Earth is the only thing . . .

III

The Lazarus Project

for Barbara

Some things can't be explained.
Your mother's illness, for example,
or why scientists have invented a cell
phone charger that runs on urine;
Rheobatrachus silus has become the first
extinct frog to be cloned. It reproduces
by swallowing its own eggs
and regurgitating its young. You say

you don't know anyone who loves
their kids but doesn't regret having them.
I babysit for a friend on her birthday;
by 3:00 a.m. her daughter's eyes are flickering
street lamps at the mouth of the alleyway
leading into sleep. At 4:00 a.m. her mother calls.
"I'm in the middle of sucking this guy's cock."

Love is a black horse named Falada
who has seen too much.

When you worked at the amusement park
you were the first to find the man on the bench
at twilight. He'd blown his head open
with a shotgun, looking out over
the city. You said it was beautiful,
the view. You saw the leaves
weighted down by his remains,

99

the tree that didn't move to stop him
or get out of the way.

We drink bourbon and
it's a wonder our stories
don't end with the breath;
they go on into the night like wars,
satellites, and naked bodies
who give up their bodies
to the rain.

How elusive we can be, even to our own
skin—the doctors are playing Marco Polo
with the gene in your mother cannibalizing her
brain. They say it's like Huntington's Disease,
but not. I say Science is the future's mythology;
we just don't know where it ends.

> I'm thirty and afraid
> it's genetic, you say. I've been scared
> of everything since puberty,
> I've only ever slept with one man and
> I feel grotesque, like Alice Hindman.

You took photos, black and whites,
for ten years, of your mother's illness.
It settled into her like the stain of a tannic wine
on snowy cloth. Everything she was, taken—

her blonde hair and beauty—everything
taken but her voice. I dream of the head
of that horse nailed to the drywalled sky.
What would it say to the body?

    She's not my mother.
    I don't even love her anymore.

Flipping through your portfolio I am struck
by the image of her hand, wrinkled over
an ashtray. How she smoked, but now
can't even close the dishwasher
on her own. Your father yells at her for things
she can't remember. When she had the first seizure
years ago he wishes he'd let her die.
And if she only knew,
how the heart would rue. Sometimes,

being alive is overwhelming. Sweat
is the skin telling our story without blame.

    The only thing that gets me through
    is reminding myself our sun will die.

I finish the bottle of bourbon and try to talk
of other things: what we are—asterisms
in this endlessly finite funnel of vein and bone.

We are dour because it's easy
being inebriated alone. It only rains
when we aren't looking up into the sky,
faith working its way into the shoulders
like clams into burrows of rock.

Why defend the dolorous?
A coworker emails to say he's leaving his wife
for you, but you didn't ask for this. You asked
why people call this giving up, because
if you do have your mother's illness you'll live
longer than she will. You like movies
and music, swimming in the ocean and making art.

That's enough.

Even Science is starting to believe
we might actually be alone, each black hole
holding another system
in its heart. At its center, another
void with its own possession of stars,
an endless tunnel. We are barreling through
the universe like a slug. We may never know

resurrection outside the sacred walls of
this test tube. Our bodies
overflow with whiskey and other things

we cannot understand, like
love. I bought you flowers
to replace the bourbon. I left them
on the liquor shelf.
Try not to let it wreck you.

Pixel Sky (Interior)

Alex is in the bathroom getting high. For hours
we play   with each other
    spin the cell phone

I do not want you. Blue body
of morning—yes your fingers are heavy—
    bring in the light, with
touches along the dull coat of an eggshell.

Another conclusion:
   Of time and how it moves like thought.

Of plastic spinning   fluid on leaves
               lighter
numbers rotating
            this moment with blame.

Or the reverse. A voice
Talking backwards through wire. I remember
the cups and the twisted bobby pins between them.
    We are always thirteen . . .

Pixel Sky (Interior)

You want to be a phone sex operator. Say,
your dad keeps all the digital women
on the top shelf. You've been lonely. We talk
through the Styrofoam speaker until you fall asleep.

I feel as if I am in my own house, miles away and cold,
so cold, I forget
        . . . though we are in the same room . . .

Pixel Sky (Interior)

They called it a house, the sky. Said
they loved most the acoustics, how
we are all under the same roof when the weather falls.
They called it the patchwork of heaven. I said

imagine being older, your job is
to nail stars to the sky. You should
nail the sky to sides of our house

So everyone could live there.

Pixel Sky (Exterior)

Only once did you find me in the woods, and even then
it was not the interior you were looking for.
By accident we stumbled upon an opened deer
and you wanted to talk of love;
its making. Everything was red, down to the bone-tip
of your finger, pointed at me like a gun.

Insomnia Poem

1.
Ashley has two children with names.

She had a baby in high school,
when we all thought she'd never lose her virginity.
I check my email at four in the morning
to find that one child is six, and I feel
I'm going blind. I take more vitamins
than I have teeth. I can't sleep
more than two hours a day. It's always 2004,
my grandmother is dying:
Aunt Marion cries,
It's just not her. I don't know how

I'll bury my mother.
All I have are my hands,

pushpins to keep a sheet over the window:
it's night forever if I don't walk outside—
remember:

It's Sunday. I'm alone
in my body.

2.

Trina was pregnant too,
for a while. The rumor is still that
she threw herself down the stairs:
she couldn't afford the abortion.
It was her "happy accident," like
the fifth cigarette I put out on my arm before
jumping into oncoming traffic.

The rumor is
deaths come to us, like ideas
in the shower, but I couldn't wait.
I knocked my head against that door,
dumb as a woodpecker. I carried my grief
like a child huddled and shivering
in the belly of a nightmare

for a while: I kept my word. Portia,

listen, a note pinned to the collar,
a mangy, wandering dog. I slept
in the corner of my body, afraid
the light was a vicious, hungry animal
that flaunted
my voice.

The things people said:
depression isn't real.
You're too damn smart
to feel this sad. You have to make it up,
the time you've missed, the reasons
you're trying to leave. The Lord

God will guide you back.
God, how could you do this
to your poor family? God,
you're being so selfish.

     God,

        God—

I was expecting you to bring me jeans,
my Spider-Man shirt, not the blinding orange
Bible, pages thin as the voice of L., who is still always
hanging herself in the early conversations of birds
in the room across the hall as I dream. Some truths burn

like houses and the people who run back into them.

Zeitgeist

for Jonathan

You are the assassin. You are
also the head that rolls near his feet,
a hubcap spinning in the street after
the world's most beautiful suicide. Let's say
it's 1947. You step out of your rib cage and into the sky.
No one sees. You decide not to leave a note
though you know it's a long way down,
and who could you tell that wouldn't think this
a choice, selfish all the same?

You were born to hold a gun, grow a beard
furrowed as the bark of a chestnut tree,
though you say you were born to push out grandkids
for your father, bring home a man
who would take care of you: his voice,
beams of light at dawn, smoothing
the winter hills.

* * *

Even the dead hear this sound: the crash,
your body folded into something
you were never supposed to be;

You're trying

to put yourself back together,
as if you'd ripped up the manuscript,

realized the next morning it was the only thing
in your life worth keeping. The fragments:

    February. A wolf outside your window.
    A messenger. Gun in the lockbox.
    Estrogen shots. HRT. Reading
    Eliot to your wife's swelling belly.

                * * *

    April. Stares at the bar. Stares
At the supermarket. Whispers.
    Fag. Tranny.

Threats. Cell phone pictures
snapped by a stalker.
No muscle to fight anymore.
    they stitched my cheek to my jaw
No muscle to fight anymore.

                * * *

You remove your pictures from the internet,
The record of transformation erased.
Only the mirror: your doctor, your wife.   Your mother
who can no longer look you in the eye.

Her prayers are like the drumming of the Carthaginian Priests
which grew louder during sacrifice
to smother both mother and child's echoing pain.

You hand her your head.
It is her own.

    Breast and scrotum.
    Perineum. Crown.

Love in the Time of Revolution

for Scott

Listen, I know you're lonely.
I can see it in the way your hair curls down
over your forehead, the slump of your shoulders
as you bend to take a hit from the bong
you spent the weekend cleaning, like a pistol.

And it takes the night being ravenous,
rejections at the bar
and you being shitfaced to admit
through bloated eyes that you are human,
         just wanting to be held
         by a woman who loves you.

Believe me, nothing inside the body is ever quiet:
the heart whispers in its sleep, even
when the lips are closed. Blood chases itself
like a child down a labyrinth of veins
like the water that recycles itself
through the lakes and marinas in Montana—

some processes can't end. Even after love
the body keeps stretching, is filled with things
that move. My hairs stand on their own at the sight
of a moth, paddling circles around the foam
in a single unwashed bowl in the sink.

* * *

To love
      you say
            It will happen on its own
like drops of rain making a map on the window
or a baby, suddenly aware
      of its hands, exploring the freedom
of a fist.

Know that even as you read this you are envied
by the cholla, which, if it could think, would
believe that we can touch each other

without pain. I won't lie—
you cut the San Pedro, boiled it into a soup,
strained the needles from the meat
and you called it medicine.
We drove for hours and I recalled
reading how in three hundred years
if it's left untouched, the cactus will
finally show its bones.

We drank at noon,
the sun eyeballed us with suspicion
knowing we have so much more choice
in how we rise and fall. I felt nothing
      but jealousy for the falcon, that
            talking spirit that would not

abandon the sky, committed four hours
to tracing its name on the open palm of blue
so someone would know it was there.

And we do the same. I counted the plastic bottles
John collected along the trail as we set up camp. Things
the land could not take back, like regret.

* * *

Sometimes voice is not enough. Sometimes
a word falls from us like a boulder and rolls unnoticed

until it is dust. I must say I tried.

I felt nothing but
        the fingers of the evening resting
on my cheeks, the needles catching
on my heel and staying
like the ghost of a bog.

You left us in the circle
around the camp where the cacti danced
and died, shaking their skeletal knees
at the mountain.

What stories did they have to tell?

Nothing quite like your move to La Paz,
how in leaving you thought you would never see
Fedra again. How you loved her
without knowing her, and then she was gone.

That memory still moist
on your lips,
you met a friend of a friend during an uprising
and you found her in a city of four thousand—
you locked eyes. You kissed. You exchanged numbers
but never called her, that opportunity missed
like a train being swallowed
into a deep winter sunset.

Remedios, Flying a Kite

Beauty, today, is boxed wine,
menthol cigarettes—a cat and a pen,
the clear soprano of Joanna while I'm out on the lawn.

This is how I lift the dead
on the anniversary of my grandmother's
passing—this year that begins with an emptying sky,
everything with wings restless and sinking,
the Costa Concordia capsized off the coast of Giglio.

In the shadow of a palm I tie a cherry stem into a knot
as my roommate bends to pick a thumb-sized replica
of a Jane Austen novel from the soil of our garden.
Only the kale has survived.
The ground is hard won't sprout
a finger or thumb. I throw a clay stone over my shoulder

anyway, think of my mother, as Deucalion,
who fathered everything after the flood.
How alone he must have been there, at the end of the world.
The freedom he must have felt throwing away the past
and starting again, the way mother believed that after a storm
the world was new.

But it hasn't rained in weeks. Bird shit dots my car,
at night when the wind shakes the city I am convinced
that soon grackles will fall from the clouds. They will come down

like bloated bodies that rise to the surface after a shipwreck,
or reverse firecrackers that explode when they hit the glass dome
of night—

New Year's Eve on the entrance to the apocalypse.
Humans being human and in heat. The discomfort
of the drunk and lonely, of having to call this home.
Everyone naked in their own eyes, everyone
the color of white rum and gin.

The screams of the crowd as they all join in.

      My skin camouflaged my exit into the dark,
the past wide as the eyes of parents straining to see me
         perform in my first play: "The Second Light of Josiah,"

All Saints, 1992.
What an angel I was. After forgetting my lines,
in that silence, giving nothing but a guilty wave
that said I caused this catastrophe.
Sweat under the stage lights and then the freedom
of being hoisted from the world by a rope.

      All those white faces smiling,
            the night sprinkling its dark feathers around me . . .

And Joanna is singing
and the sun is just tilting its head over the mountains.

And the chorus begins

again. My roommate is turning
on the water. The clay separating
like land does, or people.

After the last cigarette is ash and the wine box runs dry
and the cat has retired to bathe in front of the living room window
it is still today.

My grandmother watches me go from her room, knowing
that this is the end, like Remedios
being pulled towards heaven, taking the blanket
and the comfort from the nun.

My grandmother, always rising,
otherworldly, one hand clutching a string
that dissipates into blue

to be taken.
To want to go.

Love Poem

When I run out of ideas on ways to build a time machine, to crossbreed elephants with giraffes, I unwrap an entire bag of peppermints and stack them in shapes that I think resemble crop circles, or Inca pyramids. It is early. It is hot. People are still planning to burn Qurans. The other night I was sitting on a mountain, heard a kid say he was excited about Spider-Man on Broadway. In the paper I read about a woman who severed her pinkie in a car door, and for three hours all I could do was draw pictures of my left hand from different angles. I searched the internet for images of scar tissue, earthquakes, openings to caves. There are so many definitions for separation, so few for belief.

Abstract Infinity, Farewell

We crabwalked through the apartment, racing towards the goal
of a back massage and dinner from the loser.
You were drunk. I was bored and in the mood to let you win at anything.

The best stories are the ones that end where they begin.
We jogged around the complex shoeless, inhaling winter,
exchanging ideas about the novel we could write. The story
of being sober in a buzzing body.
    I'm still in here, you said, *I can prove it . . .*

* * *

When I was seven my friend James asked us to help him carry his dead dog from
the street. He saw the truck snatch its body and drag it two blocks. The dog died
with its eyes open, and aside from the tread marks on its stomach and the awkward
angle of its legs, he still looked healthy and alive. James couldn't tell his father. We
took the dog to the tree that marked the edge of the woods and we dug a hole with
our hands. With his pocketknife, James sawed open the poor dog's throat and
made an incision in its belly for the maggots to slide out. Stupid dog never listened,
he said. Stupid dog was always chasing cats into the street. Help me bury the
body, he said. Tommy was only four then, kept poking the carcass with his shoe.
"Where's the dog?" he kept asking. "James, where did it go?"

* * *

And from the snow comes the blanket, hood of your eyes, shadow of constant warning.
And from the sky comes mildew, warnings of constant shadow, eyes of your hooded
blanket, the coming snow.

* * *

You surrender to the comfort of warnings;
if there was drool on your mother's mouth in the morning, or a paper cut or ache,
you made for the doctor—an appointment with the intellect of colors, fashion of
pills you lined next to the sink in the frail shape of a grin. Nothing escapes
in capsules. Nothing confines like powder.
"How awkwardly we're crammed in these bodies," you said.
        And still, and still . . .

* * *

The bar closed and I stood, waiting
        for an exit. Near the door
a woman with a Spanish accent cringed
when she saw my nose ring, asked me if it still hurt.

In Mexico it's not acceptable for men to have piercings.
She said it is *weird*, it looks painful and it is weird.
I had not touched a glass, but feigned drunkenness, told her,
"Actually I have a disease and the piercings,
    they keep me from bleeding.
    It's kind of like plugging a drain."

Her eyes were heavy and I could tell she believed me.
"Go on," I said. "I'm just metal and bone. Try to pull it out."

But it looks weird, she protested, it looks *weird.*

"I'm still in here," I said.

Notes on the Poems

"My Girlfriend Recaps the News"

James Craig Anderson was a forty-seven-year-old African American man who was murdered in a hate crime in Jackson, Mississippi, on June 26, 2011. Having lost his keys, Anderson was in the parking lot of a motel attempting to access his car when he was beaten and robbed by a group of white people led by eighteen-year-old Deryl Dedmon of Brandon, MS. It's reported that earlier that evening, Dedmon suggested to his friends, "Let's go fuck with some niggers," before the group drove to the Westside of Jackson in search of a target. Though the attack was not captured on the motel security camera, it did show Dedmon running over Anderson with his pickup truck, which ultimately caused his death. Dedmon was later documented on numerous occasions as having bragged to his friends afterwards: "I ran that nigger over."

"The Lazarus Project"

The title borrows its name from a group of Australian researchers at the University of New South Wales, who themselves were inspired by the biblical account of Lazarus of Bethany, a man claimed to have been resurrected by Jesus four days after his death. The aim of The Lazarus Project is the de-extinction of animals via cloning. In 2013 the group successfully cloned embryos containing DNA from the previously extinct Australian gastric-brooding frog and their future goals include reviving the Tasmanian tiger, the dodo, the passenger pigeon, and the woolly mammoth.

The black horse Falada is a reference to the 1815 German fairy tale "The Goose Girl," in which a princess is sent by her widowed mother to marry the prince of another land, given only a servant, a handkerchief or lock of hair (depending on the Grimms' version of the story you read), and a magic talking horse for her journey. Halfway to their destination the slave girl threatens the princess and steals her clothes and identity, forcing her to take an oath to never divulge what has happened. Once they arrive the slave girl presents herself to the king and prince as though she were the princess, and they believe her. Upon realizing that the talking horse, Falada, was a witness and could potentially speak to what had happened, the slave girl ordered the horse to be beheaded. Hearing this, the princess, now acting a servant to her former slave, begs Falada's slaughterer to nail the horse's head above the entryway to the city, where she will see it as she passes with her geese every morning. In the mystical manner that makes fairy tales so engrossing, the bodiless horse does not die, and each morning the princess passes the horse greets her, stating, "Alas, alas, if your mother knew, how her heart would rue." The truth is eventually discovered, the slave girl committed to death and the princess taking her rightful place as the prince's wife, though Falada, beheaded for what she saw, never tells anyone.

"Remedios, Flying a Kite"

The first portion of the title refers to Remedios the Beauty, a character in Gabriel Garcia Marquez's novel *One Hundred Years of Solitude* who literally floats away to heaven in front of her family.

Biographical Note

Dexter L. Booth is the author of *Scratching the Ghost* (Graywolf Press, 2013), which won the 2012 Cave Canem Poetry Prize. Booth's poems have been included in the anthologies *The Best American Poetry 2015*, *The Burden of Light: Poems on Illness and Loss*, and *The Golden Shovel Anthology* honoring Gwendolyn Brooks. He received a PhD in poetry from the University of Southern California and is a contributing editor for *Waxwing Journal* as well as a professor in the Ashland University MFA program.